CLOSING THE GATE OF HELL: THE THIRD HEAVEN

Anthony Chuma Mgbogu

ISBN: 9798824132229
Independently published

DEDICATION

TO THE GOD –ALONE

PREFAC

The concept of heaven needs a very in-depth study and analysis because as it is commonly understood, it is not enough to divorce some inherent contradictions controversies as to whether heaven is a created place or condition count as one of the major issues that are verified in this book. In the same vein, hell fire by influence is critically looked into as to whether it is a place or condition applying to what and not what. Can heavenly condition as ordinarily understood as one of enjoyment and bliss be properly fit in to the arbitrary nature of man. What you desire and want is not the same with what I want. In brief, what is the nature of beings in heaven. _Another issue is the idea of time. Is heaven a time-based concept? All these things will lead one to make a very interesting study of the concepts of eternity, forever, and constant here, constant is, and constant now.

It will be interesting to the reader to find out that heaven is in stages. The different stages have different characteristics marking them. Therefore, one stage of heaven varies with another in content but agrees with it in purpose. The third heaven is the only stage of heaven where universalism is applied completely. All is in all, in everything and is everything. Everything is everywhere.

The Bible is used extensively in this book to

support ideas that are discussed. It is equally important to clarify that this book is not a prophetic one. Even as the issues that are discussed may border on the things not yet seen or felt, they are things that already exist. Therefore, the book takes information from the source of facts of already existing things, known and not known through revelation. prophesy is the art of foretelling things that not yet there, and which has the possibility of not coming true. If it happens, then it is a true prophesy but if not, it becomes a false prophesy. Revelation can also be about something that is systematically put in place such that it will manifest itself in one form or the other in the future. It can equally be about a thing destined or designed by God to take place in the future. Revelation is therefore are about real things. Knowledge in all aspects continues to be enriched by revelation.

By reading and meditation on the averments of this book, one can find himself on a very magnitude where he can position himself on the echelon required for him to discover himself. One will then come to know who and what he is, where he is and where he is going. Anyone who has a problem with any postulation in this book can take recourse to the author for more clarification. May the almighty God continue to guide us.

Mgbogu Anthony Chuma
08062666975

ACKNOWLEDGMENTS

My thanks go to my darling wife Mrs Ebere Mgbogu A, my children Chidimma, Chinwe, Chisom, Chidiofu, Uzochukwu, and Udeoma for their assistant in the research and typing of this work. In no small way also, my thanks go to Akachukwu. In a very special way, I thank brother Humphery Akaolisa for his selfless contribution in terms of time, service, resources, and technical assistance in getting this work published.

Anthony Mgbogu
08062666975

CHAPTER 1

THE CONCEPTS OF ETERNITY AND FOREVER

Eternity and forever are two words that often used interchangeably. In many occasions especially in most religious literature the words appear in reference to time. The two words are related to time calculations the place of time in human relations and history is so important that one cannot put it aside in deciding the fate of future events. And in most cases, the idea we hold of the future determine what we do presently. Because concepts of eternity and forever are time related, they will be critically examined within the purview of time so as to place them in their real perspective.

The oxford advanced learners dictionary of

English language defines eternity as time without end. Also, forever is defined as a life time beyond the grave. The emphasis in the above meaning is on every long time.' one can therefore without hesitations suggest the two concepts is to means a period of time beyond imagination. Can there be really a time without end?

Time is a creation. Before the creation of the phenomenal regulators of time like the sun, the moon, the earth, and other related planets, there was no idea of time, therefore the meaning of time can only be found within the present created order. It is these regulators that give us the phenomenal appearances and orders of day and night and which are broken into seconds, minutes and hours, leading into days, weeks, months, and years. The collapse of these regulators will therefore lead us to the dawn of timeless era. By this is meant an Era of no time. There will be no time to calculate. Therefore, the will be no idea of a time calculated into a countless magnitude. The concepts of eternity and forever can therefore only be defined as the period of time lasting from the death or expiration of the normal life activities of a thing to the end of time.

When the two concepts are used in the Bible it will be properly understood that the emphasis is to the length of time long enough that nobody knows when it will end. It is a period surpassing a life time far into the future, for as long as there is created life of this present order. What had been before creation does not fall within the concepts of forever and eternity nor what will be at the end of all existence that is at the termination of all that enjoy God's present created nature. A few Biblical references will help to explain further the concepts of eternity and forever especially as used in the Bible. The concept was captured very well in the gospel of **Mathew 25 31-46,** it says "when the son of man comes as king and all the angels with him, he will sit on his royal throne, and the people of all the nations will be gathered before him. Then he will divide them into two groups just as a shepherd separates the sheep from the goats. He will put the righteous people on his right and the evildoers on the left. Then the king will say to the people on the right, come you that are blessed by my father! Come and possess the kingdom which has been prepared for you ever since the **CREATION** of the world. I was hungry and you fed me, thirsty and you gave me a drink I was a stranger and you received me in your home, naked and you clothed me. I was sick and you took care of me, in prison and you visited me. The righteous will then answer him and say, when lord, did we ever see you hungry and fed you, thirsty and gave you a drink, a stranger and welcomed you? The king will reply, whenever you did this for one of the least important of these brothers of mine, you did it for me. Then he will say to those on his left, away from me, you that are under God's course. Away to the **ETERNAL** fire which has been prepared for the devil and his Angles. I was hungry but you would not feed me, thirsty but you would not give me a drink, I was a stranger but you would not welcome me in your home, naked but you would not cloth me. I was sick and in prison but you would not take care of me. Then they will reply him, when lord, did we ever see you hungry, or thirsty, or in prison or a stranger, or naked, or sick, and would not help you? The king will answer, I tell you whenever you refuse to help one of these least important ones, you refuse to help me. These then will be sent out to **ETERNAL PUNISHMENT** but the righteous will go to **ETERNAL LIFE.**"

Eternity from the above quotation is clearly explained by Jesus as of a product of creation. It was created along with the world and meant for the righteous. As a product of creation, it cannot outlive creation. Eternity as enjoyed by those who merit eternal life is the second stage of heaven or what can be simply referred to as the second heaven. Eternal damnation is also commonly referred to as the second death. The concept of the second heaven will be fully discussed later in this work. The determinant feature of eternity, time, and place, are in themselves subject to termination and so is eternity.

The biblical reference of **Rev. Chapter 4:1-11**, will be used to explain very well the concept of forever, it says, "At this point, I had another vision and saw an open door in heaven. And the voice that sounded like a trumpet which I had heard speaking to me before said, come up here and I will show you what must happen after this. At once, the spirit took control of me. There in heaven was a throne with someone sitting on it. His face gleaned like such precious stone as jasper and carnelian and all-round the throne there was a rainbow the colour of an emerald. In a circle round the throne were twenty-four other thrones on which were seated twenty-four elders dressed in white and wearing crowns of gold. From the throne come flashes of lightening, rumblings and peals of thunder in front of the throne, seven lighted torches were burning which are the seven spirit of God. Also, in front of the throne, there was what looked like a sea of glass clear as crystal.

Surrounding the throne on each of the sides were four living creatures covered with eyes in front and behind, the first looked like a lion, the second looked like a bull, the third had a face like a man's and the fourth looked like an eagle in flight.

Each one of the four living creature had six wings and they were covered with eyes inside and out. Day and night, they were singing, holy holy holy is the lord God Almighty who was, who is, and who is to come. The four living creatures sing songs of glory, honor, and thanks to the one who sits on the throne.

Who lives **FOREVER AND EVER**. When they do so, the twenty-four elders fall before the one who seats on the throne and worship him who lives **FOREVER** and **EVER,** they throw their crowns down in front of the

Throne and say our lord and God, you are worthy to receive glory, honor, and power, for you created all things and by your will they were given existence and life".

A Good look at the above text reveals certain glaring details about the concept of forever. Day and night are features of the created order by God. John the beloved apostle was shown this vision when he was still alive, and we believe the bible in all respect of this account. Day and night the twenty-four elders were seen surrounding the throne of God and singing praises to him continuously implies that they are in the act of singing praise without end, to the end, after a very long time leading if possible, beyond death. Death here could apply to the termination of all humanity obviously, God will always be, but created things or forms in their individual identity will not always be. Certainly, whatever has a beginning has an end. All thrones including the ones mentioned in the above text are product of creation. The phasing out of all manner of creation will certainly bring to an end the concept of forever in relation to the event, therein. Thrones as well as all creation will certainly pass away leading to the actualization of time less era. Development in the above text can only be properly located within the ambit of second heaven.

The concept of eternity and forever are therefore similar in major respect as used in the bible. So long as they relate to time, they do not transcend beyond the ambit of second heaven. Before creation, there was no idea of time irrespective of length. But before creation, there was God in all aspect of his Goodliness.

CHAPTER 2

THE CONCEPT OF CONSTANT IS, CONSTANT NOW, AND CONSTANT HERE

The three concepts of constant are, Constant now, And Constant here are interwoven together even as they are different from one another. Each of them will be explained in its proper perspective while throwing light to the other concept. A study of the concept is very important because a good understanding of them will enable one appreciate in a good measure the true position of things as it relate to the issue of the third heaven. The above three concept bother on the three existential dimensions of identity, time, and space. And since they are all subject to termination, what will be the state of things at the final end of things. This study therefore helps to find out if there is anything that is constant, and which subsists and sustain the ever flux state of things, that is created by nature. Let's take them seriatim

THE CONSTANT IS.

The concept of constant is relating to the reality of a thing. It bothers on the fact of the existence of a thing. It goes to explain how a thing or being unyields to another other than partaking into a union with another while remaining itself in enriching the union by what it really is. Created things are obviously subject to changes but there are things which determine them and which when they remain themselves are unyielding to changes. These actually are live souls. Since live souls will therefore survive changes and the end of all things, it invariable become the arena for the study and understanding of the nature and position of existential realities. In otherworld's, what is the character and mode of existence of all or anything that survive the end of time and creations generally. All the changes that occur in creation are instituted by God, through the two major principles of LACK and GULLABILITY. One can change to something because there is that which he lacks, that he does not have. As far as an existent lack one character or the other in itself either by complete absence or by measures of quality and quantity, then an open possibility of changes has been created. However, this open possibility cannot translate to changes in identity without gullibility. It is because it is possible for things to yield themselves to another thing that makes things change. Things wish to become what is possible for them to become under given circumstances. And when the circumstances are applied, they succeed in the change of their identity even things which never wished or wanted to change their identities can have them changed for them by others because they cannot safe guide themselves against external influence. They are therefore gullible to factors that act on them and change their identities therefore all the actions and changes that occur among things are instituted by God but off course not always and directly effected by God.

But God is not lacking in anything, either by quality or quantity. And there is nothing that can forcefully and externally influence on God as to be able to change him. God therefore can only change himself to us by way of information that is, enabling us to know that of him which hitherto we knew not, but not by either reduction or addition of quality and quantity. The change of God is there for not a characteristic one but an informative one. However, this informative change of God contributes to our own characteristic change. God therefore enriches creation by opening up certain aspect of himself to us continually by way of sight, hearing, in sight through meditation, etc. the information must be about real things since God is real, but it must not be concreted or physical things since material things are ephemeral it can be either abstract or material provided it is about something that really is. Deceptive changes are those that route from false phenomena, things that are never there, generally introduced to us by deceptive agents. When this occurs, it tends to thwart the rise in human knowledge and excellence in creation. Because this changes route from false phenomena they do not qualify for any identity. Their source, do not exist. In the same vein, because material things are ephemeral, they do not qualify for any identity that will survive time.

At the end of time, what truly will exist is that

which is of God and is no longer under-going changes. It remains in its singular and constant identity. There are uncountable numbers of these existences more as there are multiple numbers of creations. Each of these existence' lack nothing and therefore is not gullible in terms of what is desired or wanted and therefore cannot force or be forced into a union and or changes. Decision and volition guide the entire operational system. Each gets what it needs from the other, or one another while remaining its true self. Aptly put, a need of any type can only be determined by collective decision just also as the answer or supply thereto. There is no hidden knowledge or information since every existing thing are available and open to all. Everything is clear 1st john 3vs 2 in this realm, there is no struggle for supremacy because all are equal in capacity even as all are not the same in identity. The collective identity of all existence which is the sum of the identities of all the existence is always the same. Therefore, at the end of time, God and those in God will always be, and in their form lacking nothing. They will translate into the "Be" or "Is".

THE CONSTANT NOW

Constant now is a time related concept. As already explained, day and night, two major operators of time are ephemeral; implying that time is bound to come to an end. Time as presently experienced is a created thing and will equally elapse with creation. Time exists for the rationalization of a process, events, changes and accountability. Process is the systematic way of doing something, the stage by stage of getting something done. Apart from processes, there can be instant events which happen either randomly or regularly and which need the concept of time for rationalization. Changes that occur in the nature and state of things both in quality and quantity are possible of explanation because there is time. This passing time with all its features will ultimately be absorbed by the more lasting aspect of existence of the timeless era or constant time, the constant now. Even as the earth and creation generally has time for its regulation, the system does not apply to God who exists outside time. Within the realm of God, time goes into extinction to give way to a different governing order.

In heaven, there are no processes, event, changes, and accountability as occasioned by lack or what it needs. Event and activities of any sort can only take place only as a matter of the will of God. This is because; whatever is in heaven has gotten to a state of complete self-realization or actualization and expression. There is no needful activity except the act of being; it is this act of continuous being and self-sustainability without changes that is aptly captured in the concept of constant now. There is no yesterday, no today, and no tomorrow. Whatever exists, exists in the ever present now. The state of constant now should not be misconceived to be a state of complete inactivity or dormancy because the act of being which is exercised by the respective existence is the most realistic form of activity. It is this form of activity that each and every live soul exerts and contribute in maintaining the existing network. Every other aspect of work or activity gets its enablement from this all consistent network. Anything in heaven knows of itself and other existents thereof, not as existing as of a time to another time. It knows and sees the entire reality or being or existing from no time to no time; the constant now.

THE CONCEPT OF CONSTANT HERE

The concept of constant here is related to space. The earth as characterized by material and non-material dimensions as provided by the prevailing space is a creation and as such is subject to an eventual end. space is created to serve a purpose on earth. By the time, it would have done with its purpose or the time when existence would not require its need, then space will be no more, especially as it is presently constituted. On earth, the major material factors of space include the crust and the sky. It is these two dimensions of space that help to determine the location and feature of different places and things. All life forms and developments on earth are availed by the provision of space. By space too, the two systems are maintained to provide nourishment to the different life form on earth. Acquisition and maintenance of property is made possible by space. The above few purposes of space only shows that space is created to serve the purpose of man on earth. The terminal end of the earth with all its features, including space will therefore lead to a state of another concept that last for time. All that exist to form space is very much given to changes. Atmosphere and environment change very often.

In the third heaven, the structural idea of space gives way to the concept of constant here, with its different characters. Existents in the third heaven do not have any need of structural support, biological sustenance, activities of movement, etc. In the third heaven, when the earth and the firmament would have fissile out, the major determinants of space will no longer be there to play their role and as such an entirely different scenario will be obtained.

In the third heaven, individual existence will occur only in the form of live souls while there will be only one corporate existent: God. A live soul just as God is its own space. The network in the system afford a particular live soul the access of all that obtain in God while at the same time reserving to itself that which it particularly is. All the live souls exhibit this character and by that guarantees the attribute of omnipresent nature of God. A live soul just like God knows no distance because it does not need to apply movement to get what it wants. Distance as an element of creation therefore does not survive creation. Everything sees every other thing within itself and in itself, 1st john 3vs2 it is self-sustainable, thereby sustaining all. It is this system of existence that all in heaven enjoy in God. God therefore become the sole existence in the third heaven. This state of a live soul having all, seeing all, knowing all, in the absence of distance and movement give rise to the concept of constant here (John 14vs10__).

In the present state of heaven where and when heaven co-exist with space and other material and structural creations, a different operational system is obtained. Space, the earth, and all creations, are but a very infinitesimal expression of the faculties of God. They are always in the live soul in heaven even as they do not benefit from the absolute supply of the network therein; they are allowed the network relatives to their respective mode of existence.

This brief study of the three concepts of constant is, constant now, and constant here reveals in a great way that things of material dimensions, that is created things generally will not only last for a short while but have lower value than the things in heaven. It also shows that when we want to be close to God or approach him in prayer, we must have to conform ourselves to the state of God, by staying quiet, and motionless, that is without distraction. This is the most appropriate way of getting to interact with God in prayer, because to be in heaven is to get to that state of being where and when one is completely yoked with the being of God, any prayer made to God through any of the saint of God is invariably routed to God. It also explains that in the present circumstances of creation, God is not equally present everywhere, God is present everywhere at the same time but not in equal degrees. The unequal presence of God at different places will continue to be the order of things until it gets to the state of constant here when God will be the same everywhere and always. This is the state of having all, seeing all, knowing all which does not elude anything that exist.

This explains the mechanism for the different levels of anointing of God

in different places and persons. The variable presence of God in different places and time is the deciding factor in the existence of the different levels and type of heaven.

CHAPTER 3

THE FIRST HEAVEN

Heaven can be explained as a place, situation, or state of absolute comfort experienced by a being. A state or situation that is devoid of any lack being guaranteed by prevailing existential factors. These existential factors could be found either in a place or thing provided that the being or thing for which it is meant experiences or enjoys it. Therefore, the provision of these factors or ingredient of comfort is particular to a being since different individual receive different level of comfort from same condition. Individuals react differently to the same treatment of favor or punishment. Therefore, a particular condition of comfort to a person may turn out to be excess or inadequate comfort to others. And obviously, an excess or inadequate comfort graduates to discomfort. Different individual has different capacities and attribute that exist in them and which yearn for satisfaction and realization in their arbitrary choices of comfort in varying degree and values. So long as heaven in its concept of a situation or state of absolute comfort is meant for man in his created order or separate existential entity, it must be in stages. Therefore, there are three major stages of heaven.

The first heaven incorporates two kingdoms of God. The kingdom of God on earth and the kingdom of God in the immediate hereafter. The hereafter here is meant the kingdom of God applying to the dead which runs simultaneously with the kingdom of God on earth, and terminates at the end of the present earth. This is the first heaven. One most important thing about the first heaven is that it is a creation. The two kingdoms are products of God creation. Therefore, they have limited and varying features of provisions. For an indebt study of the first heaven, some excerpts will be taken from the Holy Scripture.

In the gospel of Matt 6:9-13 the lord taught us

on prayer when he said;

9.   "our father who art in heaven, hallowed be thy name.

10.   Thy kingdom come, thy will be done, on earth as it is in heaven.

11.   Give us this day our daily bread,

12.   And forgive us our trespasses as we also forgive those who trespass against us

13.   And lead us not into temptation, but deliver us from evil"

Also, in Matt 22:23-33, it was recorded as follows;

23.   The same day, the Sadducees came to him, who say that there is no resurrection and they asked him a question,

24.   Saying, "Teacher, Moses said that if a man dies, having no children, his brother must marry the widow, and rise up children for his brother."

25.   Now, there were seven brothers among us; the first married, and died, and having no children left his wife to his brothers,

26.   So, to the second and third, down to the seventh.

27.   After them all, the woman, died.

28.   In the resurrection, therefore to which of the seven will she be wife for they all

had her. 29 But Jesus answered them, "you are wrong, because you know neither the scripture nor the power of God

30.   For in the resurrection they neither marry nor are given in marriage, but are like angels in heaven.

31.   And as for the resurrection of the dead, have you not read what was said to you by God,

32.   "I am the God of Abraham, and God of Isaac, and God of Jacob"? He is not God of the dead, but God of the living"

33.   And when the crowd heard it, they were astonished at his teaching.

Also, in the gospel of Matt 25:31-46 concerning the issues of final judgment and what transpire in the thereafter Jesus said.

31.   "When the son of man comes in his glory and all the angels with him, then he will sit on his glorious throne.

32.   before him will be gathered all the nations, and he will separate them one from another as a shepherd separate the sheep from the goat. And he will place the sheep at his right hand but the goat at the left

33.   Then the king will say to those at his right hand, come, oh blessed of my father, inherit the kingdom prepared for you from the foundation of the world.

35.   For I was hungry you gave me food, I was thirsty and you gave me drink, I was a stranger and you welcomed me. I was naked and clothed me, I was sick you visited me, I was in prison and you came to me.

Then the righteous will answer him, "lord, when did we see thee hungry and feed you, or thirsty and gave you drink?

37.   And when did we see thee a stranger and welcomed thee or, naked and clothed thee?

39.   When did we see thee sick or in prison and visited thee?

40.   And the king will answer them, "truly I say to you, as you did it to one of the least of these best friends, you did it to me.

41.   Then he will say to those at his left hand, depart from me, you cursed into the eternal fire prepared for the devil and his angels".

42.   For I was hungry and you gave me no food, I was thirsty and you gave me no drink,

43.   I was a stranger and you did not welcome me, naked and you did not clothe me, sick and in prison and you did not visit me".

44.   Then they also will answer, lord, when did we see thee hungry or thirsty or a

stranger or naked or sick or in prison and did not

45.   Minister to thee?

Then he will answer them, "truly, I say to you, as you did it not to one of the least of these, you did it not to me.

46.   And they will go away into eternal punishment, but the righteous into eternal life".

The kingdom of God on earth falls in tandem with the created conditions or features on earth. The earth was created with limitations in many respects. Nothing and no one that is created to live on earth can afford to live beyond the natural provision affordable to him. The created things on earth include both the known and the unknown, seen and unseen. God created the earth to be the heaven and living place for man for a brief sojourn before ascending to the next stage of the first heaven in the hereafter. All that man needs for a life of comfort is available on earth the actual and maximum enjoyment of these provision is a different question. To be in heaven on earth does not mean the possession and enjoyment of all the provision at all times, there is always a limit to the amount of anything that would satisfy the need of it by man.

Equally, a satisfied need today may not present itself for satisfaction the next day; and in the same value and manner. Again, mere desires are outside the enjoyable provisions affordable to a person mere desires do not have an inbuilt platform for its existence in a person one who wishes to fly without the inbuilt mechanism to do so will never get to fly but can only enjoy the flight assistance of another, who has the inherent capacity to fly. In this case it is the one who can fly that is applying and enjoying the capacity to fly. In the same manner, the one with the inherent features to fly determines the maximum extent of flight that could be affordable as at a particular time, the heaven of flight to be delivered to those who need it. This calls for the principle of SHARING as the major operational system in the heaven and earth. It is not just sharing but enjoyable sharing. Another principle here is that of optimal satisfaction. To be satisfied is to be provided with what is needed to satisfy what is lacked for the enjoyment of a necessity. This is the heaven of satisfaction.

The state of heaven on earth is fully portrayed

in our lord's prayer.

The prayer is divided into three parts based on an ideal format of prayer. Despite being an ideal prayer format, the prayer targets the purpose of the coming of Jesus to earth. Jesus came to help man actualize the heaven on earth. In the first part of the prayer Jesus acknowledges God as the father, owner, and maker of all things. He also re-affirmed the constant heavenly state of God. In heaven, only God's will is done. In the second part Jesus acknowledges man as a being that has certain needs that are necessary for his survival. And in the third part, Jesus recognizes the important nature of man. Man is a being created in the order of committing errors and offending others the important and weak nature of man subject him to God for both provision and protection in all the three-part, man is subjected to God in doing his will, sustainability, and all-round protection from the pangs of sin and evil. This is not to say that man has no role to play in the enjoyment of heavenly life on earth. It clarifies that God who is the owner and giver of heavenly life on earth determines what that heavenly life is to us at different circumstances irrespective of what we may think we need and the extent thereof. It is the nature of a man's relationship with God that determines the extent he has his active and potential virtues actualized. To live with an un actualized virtue is to live outside the heaven on earth. But man, lack's the knowledge to know the virtues or attributes given to him by God for realization on earth. Therefore, when we are in good relationship with God, he supplies us with the virtues and the values that enable us to reach the heaven on earth. It is not ordinarily given to man to know when he has gotten to the limit of his virtue or personal attribute because God can improve on it. To live in the kingdom of heaven on earth is to live in the fullness of the inherent virtue with which God characterized our individual being. Even as the earth is marked with unlimited limitations, it is also blessed with infinite provisions meant to advance the course of man's life thereon. This infinite provision is creations that are waiting for exploitation by man as offered by God.

It is a common belief that the kingdom of heaven is not possible on earth. This is not true; otherwise Jesus would not have taught us to pray for the enthronement of the kingdom of God on earth. How can the lord teach us to pray amiss if what we are praying for, on daily bases cannot be granted us daily?

The second part of the first heaven is the kingdom of heaven in the immediate hereafter. Just like the first part-the kingdom of heaven on earth-the second part is a created condition and place. Whereas the provision and enjoyment of comfort in the kingdom of heaven on earth is based on relativity, as pointed out earlier, it is not so in the kingdom of heaven in the beyond.

Comfort in the kingdom of heaven in the immediate hereafter is affordable by the general creation. All that live in the heaven is able to enjoy all that are created, on need. The system in this heaven elevates the sensibilities of man such that he gets to see the entire created order and possibilities exactly the way they are and avails himself the use thereof. One in this heaven does not have automatic information and knowledge of the things that are reserved to God alone, except as offered or approved by God. Therefore, the system of network affording knowledge and use of the created orders, system, and things is applicable only to created things. Relativity here applies only to needs. One can only be supplied with what he needs and in the manner which the need will appropriately be satisfied. The struggle and the hope for this heaven conduces one for the enjoyment of the kingdom of heaven on earth. Equally, it is the life of one in the kingdom of God on earth. Even without knowing it-that qualifies one for the attainment of life in the kingdom of heaven in the beyond. Those whose lives do not conform with the established orders in the kingdom of heaven on earth, are precluded from this second part of the first kingdom of heaven.

The biblical text that was cited earlier concerning the question about resurrection, Jesus answered that in the life to come men neither marry nor are given in marriage but are like angels. This is to emphatically declare that those in the heaven, have been elevated to a higher status of existence. Marriage is a need on earth especially as captured by the questioners who understood the woman was married severally to bear children. Procreation is necessary on earth for purposes of fulfilling God's injunction to multiply and fill the earth. Angels apply the principle of bilocation or duplication to any number to serve God in circumstances of need. Therefore; they do not need to marry. It is important to note here that angels whose nature man acquires in this heaven, are themselves created by God.

In the other citation about the judgment of the just and unjust people, the good people were taken to the right hand of God to be ushered into a place, the kingdom of heaven, prepared for them from the time of creation of the earth. This part of the first heaven will obviously be brought to an end at the end of all creations. The earth and other creations will surely come to an end with time and a new systematic order of things will be ushered in.

CHAPTER 4

THE SECOND HEAVEN

The second heaven starts from where and when the first heaven stops. Just like the first heaven, the second heaven is a created one. It is a condition and place of comfort. It is characteristically different from the first heaven in some cases. In the first place, the second heaven can be in many stages or parts yet to be decided by God. It is the stage of heaven that may not have been created until now. As such, what one can understand concerning the second heaven are only those things that are offered in the scripture and through revelations. It exists in God to be delivered for use at the proper time. while the first heaven is majorly a state of activities involving men and angels, the second heaven is majorly a place of constant and steady worship of God. This is made possible because the second heaven is only part of the creations that obtain in God. God is still beyond the creation as experienced by the creature in the second heaven. The three concepts of constant is, constant now, and constant here, cannot be actualized in the second heaven. As such it is still a place of imperfect existence. There are created things that exist outside other created things and are so separately identified such as, thrones, angels, man, and animals of different kind. This is not the state of everything in everything. Again, in the second heaven, time is known and wanted. The end of the present agents of time like the moon and sun, and other animal time keepers like the cock, will only give place to other phenomena time keepers of like-nature. The second heaven is a higher level of existence in term of the ascendance to Godly state because it involves more created things and possibilities than the first heaven. The partakers will see what had not been seen before, know what had not been known before and do what was not possible of being done before. But still, they must operate within the limit of created possibilities. The things that sustain and obtain in the first heaven will totally vanish with the earth and an entirely new created order will usher in, the second heaven.

In **Mark 13:24-28** Jesus in the eschatological discuss said, "But in those days after that tribulation, the sun will be darkened, the moon will not give

Its light, the stars will be falling from heaven, the power in the heaven will be shaken, and then they will see the son of man coming in clouds with great power and glory, and then he will send the angels and gather his elect from the four wings, from the end of the earth to the end of heaven". And in **verses 30-31** Jesus said, truly I said to you this generation will not pass away before all these things take place. Heaven and earth will pass away but my words will not pass away". Also, in the gospel of **Matt .24** and **Luke 21**, the discussion of the end time and the activities or factors leading to that was explored by Jesus Christ. **Matt 24:14** clearly stated the obvious end of the earth and the first heaven. The end that is stated therein is not that of the entire existence but that of the present phenomenal existent earth. It is very important to point out that the second heaven can come into many unknown part or types depending on

God's decision, God can decide to create and recreate the earth and the order of humanity for as many times as he wants and also for any length of time that pleases him. In **Rev 20:1-15** it was a thousand years that one order of the second heaven is to take in this context, a thousand year would mean a very long time. Then the second stage of the second heaven commence thereafter to last for as long as God decide to sustain the order of creation. One particular feature of the second heaven irrespective of the stage or type is that it is always an advance state or order of life to the first heaven. Enlistment of candidate into it is purely on judgment by God using the book of life and death. Those whose name appear in the book of life should be granted life and into the second heaven while those whose names are written in the book of death are thrown into hell. Good ones who could be living as at the time of final judgment would not need to die but would have their nature transformed and taken by the angel of God into the second heaven. Also, those who had died before the day of the final judgment, I mean the good ones, will take up their bodies' again in what is referred to as in **Rev.20:1-15** as the first resurrection, to be ushered into the particular stage of the second heaven.

Rev.21 talks about the emergence of the new earth, and the new heaven. This new earth and heaven have entirely new and different features from the previous one. The structural design of the cities in it especially of the new Jerusalem and the throne of God where given in the book of revelation. The length and the width together with the doors and ornamental artifacts or the holy city were described in **Rev 21** there will be no constellations in the new heaven and earth because Jesus will serve as it source of light. As such, there will always be light available to everyone. In one aspect of the second heaven, God is to replicate the earthly features of the previous earth like vegetation, water, and animals of different types, though in different natures. Man, beast, and animal of different types will be co-existing harmoniously. Man will no longer be subject to sin because he will be made in the form of sinless nature. **Jer.31:30-34.**

The second heaven, though a place of higher values and existence, it does not give complete Godly existence and comfort. It provides full comfort to the inhabitants in a relative form. Each gets full supply of whatever virtue it needs. Again, it is a state of higher value because it provides the occupants the power to access from creation what they could not otherwise be able to access. It enriches the knowledge of the occupant. But because it is a created place and condition, it is still far from the state of full Godly existence. But obviously, the second heaven is a scene of new order of creation and manifestation of God's power.

The second heaven is a stage in the heavenly development that is created by God for him to showcase his powers. As such, it is not known, the many types of created second heaven that will take place before the proceeding to the next stage of third heaven. At each end of any particular type of second heaven, God may decide to embark on a fresh creation of phenomenal existence. God, the doer of new things, may keep pulling out of himself the infinite varieties of the worlds that exist in him.

Woe and really woe to those who are not enlisted in the second heaven because of the extent of their unbearable suffering and the time thereof. The question is not that of continued creation of new world but that of sustainability of the present created souls for purpose of either favour or punishment more so, the unveiling and continued existence of the second heaven does not in any way hinder the operations in the third heaven. But a successful conclusion of the second heaven will completely mark and end to the present order of creation and its products.

CHAPTER 5

THE THIRD HEAVEN

The third heaven is the only state of heaven that is not created. It is not a created state or form. It is a Godly condition in all aspects. It is a state and condition of all possibilities, affording anything that captures imagination. The third heaven is not subject to termination.

The state of comfort in the third heaven is not relative to individual creatures unlike what it is in the first and second heaven. This is because in the third heaven what obtains is the existence of virtues or live souls is in their infinite standards, there is no finite existence. Therefore, every infinite existence enjoys everything infinitely. Secondly, there is no greater in number or capacity of anything than any others. Each has each self infinitely supplied to each other and one another. This system makes it possible for everything to have everything; amidst differences. In the third heaven, there is no individual entity, no space, and no time. The three concepts of constant are, constant here, and constant now operate fully in the third heaven, unlike in the first and second heavens. The clarity of everything becomes quite obvious. The third heaven is purely a state or condition of existence affording joyous Godly existence, to all the Godly virtues or live souls. The third heaven is akin to the state of things before the creation of the current phenomenal earth. God was himself, without form, space, and time. Then out of himself, that is the composite live soul's aggregating the power of God, he ushered out creatures of different types, magnitudes and powers. The realm from where this created thing emanated from still exists in its original form and state, even as it sustains and maintains every other thing.

The third heaven runs in two parts.

1. From creation to the end of second heaven.
2. Beyond second heaven.

1. From creation to the end of second heaven.

This governs the period referred to as eternity. This is the period that spans from creation of the earth or any creature to the end of second heaven. On creation, man together with other animal creatures, was given automatic access to the third heaven. But when man sinned and came to the knowledge of evil and good, heaven was shut out against him. Consequently, man has to earn heaven by high moral standard. By disobedience to God man lost heaven and by simple obedience to God, man stands to gain heaven; the attainment of heaven is therefore not common to all unlike other animal creatures. Man was not alone in this unfortunate faith of loss of heaven. Higher powers of principalities and thrones equally share in the loss of common and direct access to heaven. Among these are Lucifer, and his associate angels. God had to fashion out a systematic way of reconciling himself with his creatures thereby creating the heavenly states of first and second heaven paving way for the ultimate return to himself in the third heaven. The first and second heavens, being places and conditions of comfort, though in a relative capacity, should not be misconstrued as purgatory, which is a place of penance. Therefore, the first heaven, the second heaven and hell fire are periodic platforms or places and conditions created by God for purposes of the enthronement of the third heaven. While first and second heaven serve as encouragement, hell fire serves as deterrent. As the perception of this factors play out in created orders, God, the third heaven still governs all qualities and values of the things in the third heaven and can still be manifested among created order at God instant alone. But there are myriads of created values, especially in the realms of the unknown, therefore it becomes difficult to fathom out the uncreated and created values. God in his infinite love for man keeps enriching man by affording to man that which man cannot access from creation. By this action the Holy Spirit recreates the creation of God. God achieve his purpose not by any systematic order or method. Knowledge of things of the creation of God can be acquired by strict observance of the system, or method and manner it operates but that of God is not subject to any systematic order or method. Therefore, by God's instance, decision and manner, Jesus was born to open the gate of the third heaven. Before the coming of Jesus, it is not known if anybody had made the third heaven. It was Jesus who came to prepare the ground for the eventual dominion of the kingdom of the third heaven.

2. Beyond second heaven.

This is the era of "**GOD- ALONE**". Yes, the heaven for all will it ever be? **Certainly! Certainly!! Certainly!!!** When? Is it in sight? Only God knows.

Hey! Alas for those who will suffer the fate of second death and could not make the first and second heavens because their redemption into third heaven is far-fetched. May this not be the portion of anyone.

This part of the third heaven is the state and condition of total life existence. It brings all created life to an end, both of mortals and immortals. Everything completely yields to the status of live soul existence, regaining the full alertness and consciousness it possessed before creation. At the final end of every created thing: principalities, power, thrones, orders, system, etc., God will absorb into himself all that he created. It is not to say as if any creature had been outside God either by creation or expulsion, but certain elements of creation could be in God in hell. The third heaven returns life to all. The life it returns is not necessarily that of joyfulness but of a live soul regaining its real status. There is no subjection of any form, of anything to another or oneself. All are free in their free necessary service of their being to another in the maintenance of the oneness of God. To think that God cannot recollect himself, that is, be his original self, is to posit that God by creation, had shot himself beyond reconstruction. Being and living in the third heaven is the same act of sharing one with others. This provides a network of continuous harmony in the third heaven.

The bible is replete with instances of the assurance of the state of heavenly provision but let's take a few citations for further analysis. In **1 cor.15:20-28**, the bible says.

20.   But in fact, Christ has been raised from the dead, the first fruit of those who has fallen asleep.

21.   For as by a man came death, by a man has come also the resurrection of the dead.

22.   For as in Adam all died, so also

in Christ shall all be made alive.

23. But each in his order, Christ the first fruit then at his coming those who belong to Christ.

24. Then comes the end, when he delivers the kingdom to God the father after destroying every rule and every authority and power.

25. For he must reign until he has put all his enemies under his feet.

26. The last enemy to be destroyed is death.

27. For God has put all things in subjection under his feet". But when it says, all things are put in subjection under him," it is plain that he is exempted who put all things under him.

28. When all things are subjected to him then the son himself will also be subjected to him who put all things under him, that God may be

EVERYTHING TO EVERYONE.

Also, in the book of **2Cor.12:1-3,** Paul stated that: I have to boast even though it does not do any good but I will now talk about visions and revelations given to me by the lord. I know a certain Christian man who fourteen years ago was caught up to the third heaven whether in the body out of the body I do not know, God knows". And I know that this man was caught up into paradise whether in the body or out of the body I do not know, God knows and he heard things that cannot be told which man may not utter.

The two places cited above deals very well on the fact and issues of the third heaven. This is the only state of heaven that no created things or separate identities existing therein. In **1Cor.15:20 -28**, the bible stated that the arrival to this stage of heaven will be in stages. Anyone who will make the third heaven before the second coming of Jesus, can only do so by being a candidate of the first and second heaven; except Jesus who made it directly. Then at the expiration of second heaven, which nobody knows when it will be, every other created thing, orders, thrones, dominions, principalities, etc., that are qualified or not qualified to attain the first or second heaven will then be subjected to Christ that is to say be made to take their real places of value and relevance in existence, and this they can access in Jesus. This means that everything seen and unseen will be absorbed by Jesus who has the platform for all created powers. And finally, death will be absorbed by Jesus Christ. This will mark the end of all type of death, either the first or second death, Jesus Christ now in God and bearing everything will then submit everything to God, leading to a situation where everything will be God as God is everything. That is to say that everything will offer itself to every other thing just as it has every other in itself. In this state there will be no more or less of anything that exists short of God.

What obtains will be God alone.

The two episodes of **Luke.23:42-43,** and **Jn.20:17-18**, help to explain clearer the fact and feature of the third heaven. In **Luke.23:42-43** the bible says," and he said, Jesus remember me when you come into your kingdom. And Jesus said to him truly I say to you, today you will be with me in paradise". Then in **John.20:17-18**, the bible says," Jesus said to her, do not touch me for I have not yet ascended to the father but go to my brethren and say to them, I am ascending to my father and to your father, to my God and to your God, "in **Luke.23:42-43**, Jesus made a certain promise of leading this man to the first heaven on the day of his crucifixion. It was a sure promise with belief that he certainly made heaven that same day. But in **John.20:17-18,** Jesus was telling Mary Magdalene that he has not yet ascended unto the father in the third heaven. The two episodes only imply that Jesus was in the first heaven with the man on the day of his crucifixion. This first heaven is a condition applying only to those who are qualified for it irrespective of place or thing. In **2Cor.12:1-3,** Paul was given a vision of the third heaven which he saw vividly to the extent he vowed to boast of it. It was a vision of a man that was caught up in the third heaven. Explicitly, Paul was given a vision of the vistas of heavens up to the third one. He was also allowed a vision of some element of the feature of the third heaven like being in body and out of body. This vision was given by God to inform us about the existence and characters of the third heaven.

The statemen.t of Jesus in **John.20:17-18**, that mary should not hold him because he had not yet ascended to the father, brings out some glaring features of the third heaven just as the statement of Paul in **2Cor.12:1-3,** that the man he saw in the vision was either in body or out of body, does. what Mary actually saw was a vision of our lord Jesus Christ in his state of readiness to ascend unto the father. It was the real Jesus in the form of fully activated live souls. This state of live souls has a special type of network governing the system in all aspect of Godliness. In this state, physical entities yield into live souls. This network did not cover many therefore it could not be possible for many to have physical contact with Jesus. Mary was stopped by Jesus in her approach to hold Jesus because the failure in her bid would have thrown her into untold bewilderment and confusion about the reality about the resurrected Jesus Christ. The live souls of Jesus were very ready to route back to the father and take their original places successfully.

In **2Cor.12,1-3**, Paul relayed exactly what was shown to him about the man that was caught up in the third heaven, being in body and out of body. There might have been no easier way of showing the reality of the third heaven and of a place meant for man than for a man to be made to be seen in it. But immediately, the man was taken out of body indicating that the body of the man Paul saw was at that material time in an extra ordinary state,

The state of live soul complete alertness, routing back to God. Paul said this man was caught up in the third heaven, meaning that the man incidentally found himself in a situation or state he could do nothing about, though a state of full realization but not of his own accord. Therefore, what Paul saw was the vision of a man who helplessly found himself in the third heaven. The third heaven is not achievable on merit because apart from Jesus nobody is purely qualified to be in it. The third heaven is the state of existence that is for all.

It is the state and stage of home coming for all.

META DATA

DO YOU KNOW?

A. THAT physical entities, space, and time are ephemeral in nature and are bound to an eventual and compulsory end.

B. THAT earth is a created heaven.

c. THAT the second heaven is also a created place, though not yet revealed.

d. THAT the second heavens could come in rafters whereby succeeding ones could come after the destruction of previous ones by God.

e. THAT the heaven of all heavens, the third heaven, will finally come to be.

f. THAT the third heaven is not a created

place. It is the state or condition of God-Alone.

g. THAT all will to be God as God is all.

www.ingramcontent.com/pod-product-compliance
Lightning Source LLC
Chambersburg PA
CBHW070321160726
47999CB00003B/1091